# HEALING TEAS
# FOR YOUR
# BODY, MIND & SOUL

# HEALING TEAS
# FOR YOUR
# BODY, MIND & SOUL

ESTELLE CARRAZ, C.M.T, N.D

APEX PUBLISHING LTD

First published in 2003, Updated and reprinted in 2008 by
Apex Publishing Ltd
PO Box 7086, Clacton on Sea, Essex, CO15 5WN, England

www.apexpublishing.co.uk

Copyright © 2003-2008 by Estelle Carraz
The author has asserted her moral rights

**British Library Cataloguing-in-Publication Data**
**A catalogue record for this book**
**is available from the British Library**

ISBN 1-904444-13-X          978-1-904444-13-8

All rights reserved. This book is sold subject to the condition, that no part of this book is to be reproduced, in any shape or form. Or by way of trade, stored in a retrieval system or transmitted in any form or by any means, electronic, mechanical, photocopying, recording, be lent, re-sold, hired out or otherwise circulated in any form of binding or cover other than that in which it is published and without a similar condition, including this condition being imposed on the subsequent purchaser, without prior permission of the copyright holder.

Typeset in 12pt Baskerville

Cover Design  Estelle Carraz

Printed and bound in Great Britain

# The History of Tea

In 2737 B.C., Chinese Emperor Shen Nung had some tea leaves fall into his cup of hot water, the beverage he discovered would cause sensations around the world. During this time, water was always boiled for hygienic reasons. The pleasant aroma and invigorating taste had everyone drinking tea.

Japan was introduced to tea by Yensei, a Buddhist priest who immediately embraced the tea resulting in the creation of the intricate Japanese Tea Ceremony, elevating tea to an art form.

In England, tea gardens, ornate outdoor tea parties were the thing to do. Still to this day....

Russia discovered tea when ornate chests of the dried leaves were sent to Czar Alexis by the Chinese Embassy in Moscow in 1618. It became Russian custom to sip heavily sweetened tea from a glass in a silver holder. Russians also enjoyed honey or strawberry jam stirred into tea as their ethnic contribution.

To recover extensive expenses from the French and Indian War, England levied a huge tax on tea imported to the colonies, mistakenly believing the colonists were so hooked on it they'd pay anything to keep their supply coming in. Which created a revolution...

A tea plantation owner introduced iced tea to the St. Louis World's Fair in 1904. It was an extremely warm day and his hot tea booth was being passed up by the crowds in favor of cold drinks, they added some ice and there you go....iced tea was created!

"Anywhere a person cultivates tea, long life will follow"
-Eisai, a Buddhist monk, 1211 A.D.

# The Art of Tea

---

The tea bag came along as a surprise. Samples of tea at the turn of the twentieth century were given out in small silk bags and instead of opening the bags, the tea bag was being dropped into hot water by consumers.
Today tea is grown on tea estates and 70% of the tea we drink is grown in Sri Lanka, India, Indonesia, Kenya, Brazil, Argentina and China. The best climates for growing tea are those that are tropical or semi-tropical and tea can be grown on soil that is not fit for growing much of anything else.

**Today there are five basic types of tea:**
Black, Oolong , Green, White and Herbal tea, and from these five types spring over 3,000 cultivated varieties. The leaves are picked at just the right moment designated by the tea estate manager, then crushed to start the oxidation process.

Surprisingly, we drink the same tea today that Chinese Emperor Shen Nung drank the day he discovered it!

# Health Benefits of Tea

The overall research of tea is that it's the most potent health beverage ever! Recent studies in leading medical journals declare tea as a potential heart tonic, cancer blocker, fat buster, immune stimulant, arthritis soother, virus fighter and cholesterol detoxifier. Theses benefits are just to name a few. The chemicals in tea have been shown to protect the body against stomach, breast, colon, and skin cancers. It also helps to lower blood pressure, serum cholesterol, triglycerides, and normalize blood sugar.

Most of the research studies show significant health benefits in people who consumed 4 cups of tea or more daily although some studies found health benefits in those who consumed as little as 3 cups a day. Some of the most impressive therapeutic properties about green and black tea to date are on the next few pages:

# Properties of Tea

Green tea speeds up the metabolism and increases the calories and fat burned- A Swiss study showed that 3 cups of green tea caused men and women to burn 4% more energy - about 80 extra calories a day. Green tea did not increase heart rate, and the calorie burning was not due to caffeine.

Green tea decreases inflammation and development of arthritis and other conditions- Case Western Reserve University study found that the equivalent of 4 cups of green tea daily reduced the development of arthritis in rats by 50%. A UCLA study found drinking green tea reduced inflammation of the stomach that could lead to stomach cancer.

Black tea can reduce tumor growth - a Rutgers University study found that a component of black tea called TF-2 caused colorectal cancer cells to "commit suicide" reduced tumor growth in colorectal cancer. Drink tea my friends!

Black tea can lower the risk of Arteriosclerosis (clogged arteries), stroke, and heart attack - a large 10-year study in the Netherlands, found men who consumed the amount of antioxidants called "catechins" found in three cups of black tea were 50% less likely to die of heart disease, caused by narrowed clogged arteries. Another study at Boston University School of Medicine, found a 50%

improvement in heart patients with impaired blood vessel functioning (a risk factor for heart attack and strokes) who drank four cups of black tea daily.

Tea can lower the risk of viral infections-a Harvard study indicated that tea chemicals stimulated gamma-delta T-cells that bolster immunity against bacteria and viruses.

Black tea can boost immunity and reduce the risk of influenza-a Japanese study showed that gargling with black tea boosted immunity to influenza.

To promote better health drink at least 3 cups of tea a day. Note that instant, bottled, decaffeinated , highly processed or herbal teas do not have the antioxidant properties of green, black, white and oolong teas.

# Basic Types of Teas

**Black Tea:** Is the overwhelming majority of the tea consumed in the U.S. This tea is fully oxidized (dried) and produces a full-bodied brew.

**Green Tea:** Is exactly what the name suggests, it retains much of the green leave qualities because it is not oxidized. It has a somewhat delicate taste and is lighter in color. Green tea is gaining popularity in the U.S. partly because of recent scientific studies linking green tea with reduced cancer risk.

**Oolong Tea:** Is partly oxidized and is a medium between black and green tea in color and taste.

**White Tea:** Is the most delicate of all teas. The infusion produced by white tea is pale, but the flavor is full, smooth and mellow. White tea may be the best tea of all for fighting cancer. The minimal processing employed during white tea production is believed to be responsible for higher levels of antioxidant polyphenols - which are currently being studied as potential anticarcinogens.

**Herbal Tea:** While flavored teas evolve from these three basic teas, herbal teas contain no true tea leaves. Herbal and "medicinal" teas come from the flowers, berries, peels, seeds, leaves and roots of many different plants and have healing therapeutic qualities.

# Black & Oolong Indian Teas

**Darjeeling Tea:** Tippy Golden Flower Orange Pekoe
**Botanical Name:** Camellia Sinensis
Teas grown on the misty heights of the Hill District of Darjeeling, popularly known as the "Champagne of Tea" and famous the world over, for its exquisite aroma and taste. The premium Darjeeling Teas are generally mild in character and have distinctive natural fruity or Muscatel flavors.

**Assam Tea:**
Tea grown in the plains of N. E. India along the mighty river Brahmaputra and comprises a major part of the total tea produced in India. A Strong Tea with full body and strength, ideal for Milk Teas.

**Indian Green Tea:**
India also produces quality Green tea which is known to have several medicinal properties. Green Tea is grown in the plains of Dooars and now some very high quality green teas are made in Darjeeling. World famous for flavored black teas. Which is believed to relieve one from hypertension, lower blood pressure and can also be used for low calorie diets. It is a health promoting and life prolonging beverage.

**Nilgiri Tea:**
Teas grown in the South Central region of India, known

as the Nilgiri Hills or Blue Mountains.

**Ceylon Tea:**
Ceylon tea from Sri Lanka is often acclaimed as the best tea in the world. The climate of this small and exotic country is ideally suited to producing a variety of delightful flavors and aromas. Ceylon tea is a pure, high quality tea with a distinctive, rich flavor and a bright golden color.

# African Teas

**Common Name:** Rooibos Tea "Red Bush"
**Botanical Name:** Aspalathus Linearis
**Grown:** South Africa, Cederberg Mountains in CapeTown
**Properties:** Known as the "Miracle tea: in Africa.
Relieves insomnia and nervous tension, stomach cramps and colic in infants, constipation,hay fever and allergies, asthma, eases skin conditions such as eczema, acne and rashes, helps in daily supplementation of calcium, manganese and fluoride. Also helps the body's iron levels during breast feeding. It is rich in Super Oxide Dismutase ,an anti-oxidant that scavenges on free-radicals, limiting their damaging effect and thereby counteracting the body's aging process Rooibos is also low in tannin therefore not inhibiting the absorption of trace elements and minerals.

**Common Name:** Honeybush Tea
**Botanical name:** Cyclopia Intermedia
**Grown:** Mountain slopes of the Longkloof District Eastern South Africa.
**Characteristics:** Honeybush flowers emit distinct "honey" scent. In order to produce the sweetest flavor Honeybush plant is harvested during flowering season. Honeybush contains no caffeine and can be served hot or cold. Recommended steeping time: 5min.

# South American Teas

**Common Name:** Stevia Tea
**Botanical Name:** Stevia Rebaudiana
**Grown:** Native to Paraguay
**Characteristics:** Stevia is one of the most health restoring plants on the Earth. What whole leaf Stevia does both inside the body and on the skin is incredible. it is a small green plant bearing leaves which have a delicious and refreshing taste that can be 30 times sweeter than sugar. Besides the intensely sweet glycosides (Steviosides, Rebaudiosides and a Dulcoside).
**Properties:** Stevia leaf contains proteins, fibers, carbohydrates, iron, phosphorus, calcium, potassium, sodium, magnesium, zinc, rutin (a flavionoid), true vitamin A, Vitamin C and an oil which contains 53 other constituents.
**Used For:** Stevia effectively regulates blood sugar and brings it towards a normal balance. An important benefit for hypoglycemia is Stevia's tonic action which enhances increased energy levels and mental activity.Stevia is an exceptional aid in weight loss and weight management because it contains no calories and reduces one's cravings for sweets and fatty foods.

**Common Name:** Yerba Matte tea "Paraguay tea, Jesuit tea, Missionary tea & South American Holly"

**Botanical Name:** Ilex paraquariensis

**Grows:** It grows wild in Argentina, Chile, Peru, and Brazil, but is most abundant in Paraguay where it is also cultivated.

**Characteristics:** The leaves are used nutritionally and medicinally; they are usually ground and steeped in hot water for several minutes and served hot/cold.

**Properties:** Yerba Matte has numerous vitamins and minerals. There is the usual array of resins, fiber, volatile oil, and tannins that characterize many plant substances. But then there is the growing list of vitamins and minerals, including carotene, vitamins A, C, E, B1, B2, B complex, riboflavin, nicotinic acid, pantothenic acid, biotin, vitamin C complex, magnesium, calcium, iron, sodium, potassium, manganese, silicon, phosphates, sulphur, hydrochloric acid, chlorophyll, choline, inositol.

**Used For:** improves digestion to the ability to repair damaged and diseased intestines. Has the ability to quicken the mind, increase mental alertness and acuity, and do it without any side effects such as nervousness & jitters. Supplies many of the nutrients required by the heart for growth and repair. In addition, it increases the supply of oxygen to the heart, especially during periods of stress or exercise. Yerba Matte increases the immune response capability of the body, stimulating the natural resistance to disease. This also involves a nourishing and strengthening effect on the ill person.

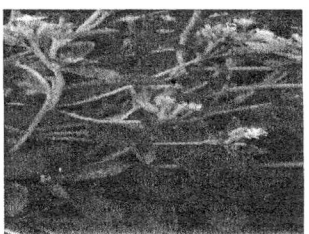

# Chinese and Japanese Teas

Japanese tea tradition dates back many centuries with some of the oldest tea companies in existence. Green tea from Japan tastes different than their Chinese counterparts. The difference is not in the tea plant, but methods of processing. The main difference is in the first step which is aimed at stopping oxidation (fermentation) where as Chinese teas are roasted over fire and Japanese teas are steamed. This process gives the tea a very delicate and delightful flavor.

**Banchas:** Are the most common and inexpensive teas; they are made of older leaves. Good quality Bancha has a sweet taste. Some of the lower grades may be bitter.

**China Green Teas:** There are many types of Chinese green teas. The most popular is Gunpowder tea. The tea leaves are rolled up into pellets resembling gunpowder pellets. Full leaf green teas are available in many grades. China white teas are young unfermented tea leaves. Young Hyson is a very popular green tea. Chun Me (eye brows) tea is produced from fine young tea leaves.

**Houjicha:** Is roasted green tea. By roasting it at high temperature, the leaf color is altered from green to red brown. This aromatic tea goes with any kinds of food, especially oily food.

**Genmaicha:** Is a blend of green tea and roasted brown rice. Light brown colored liquid with a distinctive taste similar to popcorn. Some of the rice pops during roasting process. Macha (powdered green tea) complements flavor of the rice.

**Gunpowder Tea:** It has all the health benefits of green tea with more flavor. Green tea leaves are rolled up to preserve freshness. Named due to resemblance of gunpowder pellets.

**Kukicha Twig Tea:** Kukicha is harvested from the carefully-aged twigs and stems of the tea plant. It has a unique branded full body sweetness of its own that is more often agreeable with seniors and children. After the correct aging, the twigs are toasted, providing a full-bodied tea with a hint of flavor that reminds us of nectar sweetness. Mild, and soothing, Kukicha twig tea is quite low in caffeine and can be enjoyed at any hour.
**Konacha Teas:** are referred to as powdered green teas. Please note that Konancha tea is a coarse not fine powder.

**Lung Ching, Long Jing & Dragon Green Well:** Are names for green tea produced in the famous West Lake region of Hangzhou - has delicate flavor and light - sweet aroma.

**Lung Ching Teas:** are China's "Royal Teas". Only the prime tea leaves are plucked Leaves are steamed not "pan fired" like most of Chinese teas.

**Oolong Mugicha:** (Oolong tea with roasted barley)it is entirely made from roasted barley. Next to green tea it is one of the most popular beverages in Japan. *Serving Suggestions: Pour it over ice for hot Summer – It is naturally caffeine free.*

**Puerh Tea:** A form of black tea, grown in Southwest China's Yunnan province. The mountains surrounding Puerh county which supply the leaves processed into Puerh tea. The fermentation is responsible not only for the mellow, earthy flavor, but also for its widely acknowledged medicinal properties, and the fact that rather than becoming stale and tasteless as it ages, its flavor actually develops and improves. The flavor develops more slowly through many years of natural oxidation. Fermentation meaning that, like a fine wine it can be aged up to 50 years or more.

**Sencha:** Is one of the exquisite teas with a very delicate taste and aroma. There are many varieties of Senchas with prices from a few to a few hundred dollars per ounce. In good quality tea the most important factor is processing - less steaming means retention of flavor, aroma and nutrients.

**White Tea:** White tea is similar to green tea except that it's roasted. White tea has the lowest caffeine content is very light in color and aroma.

# How to Drink Green Teas

Well, first you pick up a tea cup filled with freshly brewed green tea. Lift it gently to your lips and tilt. Make sure that the green tea in the cup is not boiling and take the tea bag out of the cup to prevent accidental choking.

## Types of Green Teas

### Japanese green teas
Teas have a very delicate natural flavor. Green tea in its purest form.

### Chinese green teas
Tea flavor is affected by pan firing - is has "smoky" taste and aroma.

### Indian green teas
A very delicate taste and different from Japanese or Chinese tea.

# How to Sweeten Your Teas

*Here are a couple of natural delicious ways to give your tea that sweet taste.*

**Honey:** Extracted from flower nectar by bees. Fructose, glucose, sucrose. Color and taste depend upon the flower source. 20% to 60% sweeter than white sugar, so use less! Honey can affect blood sugar levels, as most concentrated sugars can.

**Stevia:** Stevia is a natural, non-caloric, sweet-tasting plant used around the world for its pleasant taste, as well as for its increasingly researched potential for inhibiting fat absorption and lowering blood pressure. Add a pinch of dried leaves to your favorite tea, and it tastes like you added a spoonful of honey.

**Turbinado:** A warm, honey-colored, large crystal sugar. It melts to a perfectly smooth sheet that shatters beautifully with a light tap. Deeper and richer in flavor than fully-refined sugar, turbinado is delicious as a tea sweetener.

**Pure maple syrup:** From the sap of maple trees. Buy pure organic syrup. High in potassium and calcium.

**Maple sugar** Dehydrated maple syrup. 93% sucrose; 1% to 3% invert sugars* Organic is available.

**Barley malt syrup** Sprouted barley. Maltose, glucose, complex carbohydrates: 3% protein from malt. Dark brown, thick and sticky; has a strong, distinctive flavor like molasses. Half as sweet as white sugar. Purchase only 100% barley malt, not barley/corn malt syrup.

**Brown rice syrup** Brown rice and various enzymes. Maltose, glucose, complex carbohydrates. Amber-colored syrup with mild "butterscotch" flavor. Half as sweet as white sugar. Store refrigerated. Organic is available.

**Date sugar** Ground, dehydrated dates. Sucrose, glucose, fructose, and complex carbohydrates. Mahogany color, coarse granules. Contains folic acid. Purchase date sugar made from unsulphured, organically grown dates. Store in a tightly closed jar.

**Mixed fruit juice** Peach, pear, grape, and pineapple concentrate juice are most common. Gives you tea that extra fruity taste... very yummy!

# How to Prepare Herbal Teas

There are two ways to prepare your Herbal teas. The method you use varies depending on the herb and how strong you want the tea to be.

**Infusions:** Are used when you are using the most delicate part of the plant, leaves, the flowers seeds and fruits.

**Decoctions:** Are used to extract the harder parts of the plant, such as the roots and bark.

**General Tips to Follow:**
* Try to use a ceramic bowl or glass container (you don't want your tea to have a metallic taste from a metal container)
* Use purified water. This will make your tea taste so much better. (avoiding chemicals and chlorine from tap water).
* Bring your water to a boil before you add your herb.
* Read directions for your tea, add the exact amount mentioned.
* Make sure the lid is tight, you don't want those lovely therapeutic essential oils to escape.
* Strain your tea carefully after brewing.

# Preparing an Infusion & Decoction

**Simple Methods for an Infusion:**
* Place the herbs in a non-metal container with a tight lid and pour boiling water over them. Allow the herbs to steep for 15-20 minutes.
* If you desire a stronger more potent tea, place the herbs in a bowl of cold water. Cover with a lid and bring to a slow simmer. Remove the herbs once the boiling starts.
* Or you can let the infusion steep overnight in a jar.

**Simple Methods for a Decoction:**
* Bring water to a boil over low heat. Slowly add the herbs and allow to simmer for 15-20 minutes.
* Do not let the steam escape. Remove from the stove, strain and cool lightly before enjoying your decoction.
* Add your herbs to a pan of cold water and bring to a boil. Same as the first method, simmer for 15-20 minutes, strain it, then cool it down for your enjoyment.
* For stronger tea, follow the directions above and steep overnight.

# Angelica

**Botanical Name:** Angelica Archangelica
**Common Name:** Angelica
**Parts Used:** Roots and leaves are used medicinally, the stems and seeds are used in confectionery.
System Effected: Lungs, stomach, intestines, blood.
**Properties:** Astringent, tonic, diuretic, vulnerary, anti-inflammatory.
**Used For:** Angelica is a useful expectorant for coughs, bronchitis and pleurisy, especially when they are accompanied by fever, colds or influenza. The leaf can be used as a compress in inflammations of the chest. It content of carminative essential oil explains its use easing intestinal colic and flatulence. As a digestive agent it stimulates appetite and may be used in anorexia nervosa. It has been shown to help ease rheumatic inflammations. It also acts as a urinary antiseptic. Angelica is used frequently as a flavoring; in liqueurs such as chartreuse and benedictine, in gin and vermouth; the leaves are used as a garnish or in salads; and the candied stalks in cakes and pudding.

# Bilberry

**Botanical Name:** Vaccinium myrtillus
**Common Name:** Whortleberry, Huckleberry, Blueberry, Hurtleberry
**Parts Used:** Leaves and berries
**System Effected:** Liver
**Properties:** Astringent, diuretic, refrigerant
**Used For:** Strengthening vision, cataracts, glaucoma, macular degeneration, diabetic retinopathy, adult-onset diabetes. The leaves can be used in the same way as those of Uva Ursi. The fruits are astringent, and are especially valuable in diarrhea and dysentery, in the form of syrup. They are also used for discharges. A decoction of the leaves or bark of the root may be used as a local application to ulcers, and in ulceration of the mouth and throat.

# Blessed Thistle

**Botanical Name:** Carbenia Benedicta
**Common Name:** Holy Thistle
**Parts Used:** Aerial portions
**System Effected:** Liver, spleen-stomach
**Properties:** Tonic, stimulant, diaphoretic, emetic and emmenagogue.
**Used For:** Liver congestion, stomach problems, loss of appetite, dyspepsia, fever, bleeding, hepatitis, and jaundice. Blessed thistle is said to have great power in the purification and circulation of the blood, and on this account strengthens the brain and the memory. The leaves, dried and powdered, are good for worms. It is chiefly used now for nursing mothers the warm infusion scarcely ever failing to produce a proper supply of milk. It is considered one of the best medicines which can be used for the purpose.

# Chamomile

**Botanical Name:** Matricaria Recutita
**Common Name:** Hungarian Camomile, Single Camomile
**Parts Used:** Flower heads
**System Effected:** liver, Stomach, Lungs
**Properties:** Nervine, anti-spasmodic, carminative, anti-inflammatory, anti-microbial, bitter, vulnerary
**Used For:** A comprehensive list of Chamomiles' medical uses would be very long. Included would be insomnia, anxiety, menopausal depression, loss of appetite, dyspepsia, diarrhea, colic, aches and pains of 'flu, migraine, neuralgia, teething, vertigo, motion sickness, conjunctivitis, inflamed skin, urinary etc. This may seem too good to be true, but it reflects the wide range of actions in the body. It is probably the most widely used relaxing nervine herb in the western world. It relaxes and tones the nervous system, and is especially valuable where anxiety and tension produce digestive symptoms such as gas, colic pains or even ulcers. This ability to focus on physical symptoms as well as underlying psychological tension is one of the great benefits of herbal remedies in stress and anxiety problems. It also makes a wonderful late night tea to ensure restful sleep and is also helpful with anxious children or teething infants, where it is used as an addition to the bath.

# Cranberries

**Botanical Name:** Vaccinium Oxycoccus, Vaccinium Macrocarpon
**Common Name:** Cranberry
**Parts Used:** Berries
**System Effected:** Kidney, prostate
**Properties:** Antiseptic
**Used For:** Cranberries contain a substance which affects the acidity of the urine and acts as a bactericide. A daily cup of cranberry tea will prevent and treat cystitis, and discourage kidney stones. Fresh cranberries and cranberry beverage is used in the treatment of prostate problems, and urinary tract infections. Cranberry tea can also be used to overcome asthma attack. The berries contain an active ingredient similar to that in the drugs used to control asthma.

# Dandelion

**Botanical Name:** Taraxacum Officinale
**Common Name:** Dandelion
**Parts Use:** Root or leaf
**System Effected:** Liver, spleen, stomach, kidney, bladder
**Properties:** Diuretic, hepatic, cholagogue, anti-rheumatic, laxative, tonic, bitter.
**Used For:** Dandelion leaf is a very powerful diuretic. The usual effect of a drug stimulating the kidney function is a loss of vital potassium from the body, which aggravates any cardio-vascular problem present. With Dandelion, however, we have one of the best natural sources of potassium. It thus makes an ideally balanced diuretic that may be used safely wherever such an action is needed, including in cases of water retention due to heart problems. As a hepatic & cholagogue Dandelion root may be used in inflammation and congestion of liver and gall-bladder.

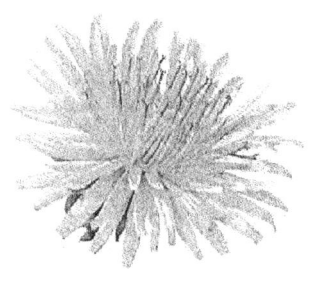

# Echinacea

**Botanical Name:** Echinacea Angustifolia
**Common Name:** Snakeroot, Coneflower, Prairie
**Parts Used:** Root, Leaves
**System Effected:** Lungs, stomach, liver
**Properties:** Anti-microbial, immune - modulator, anti-catarrhal, alterative.
**Used For:** Echinacea is one of the primary remedies for helping the body rid itself of microbial infections. It is often effective against both bacterial and viral attacks, and may be used in conditions such as boils, septicemia and similar infections. In conjunction with other herbs it may be used for any infection anywhere in the body. It is especially useful for infections of the upper respiratory tract such as laryngitis, tonsillitis and for catarrhal conditions of the nose and sinus. In general it may be used widely and safely. The tincture or decoction may be used as a mouthwash in the treatment of pyorrhea and gingivitis. It may be used as an external lotion to help septic sores and cuts.

# Elderberry

**Botanical Name:** Sambucus Nigra
**Common Name:** Black Elder, European Elder.
**Parts Used:** Bark, flowers, berries, leaves.
**System Effected:** Lungs, liver
**Properties:** Diaphoretic, alterative, laxative aged bark), stimulant, anti rheumatic (berries).
**Used For:** The Elder tree is a medicine chest by itself! The leaves are used for bruises, sprains, wounds and chilblains. It has been reported that Elder Leaves may be useful in anointment for tumors. Elder Flowers are ideal for the treatment of colds and influenza. They are indicated in any catarrhal inflammation of the upper respiratory tract such as hay fever and sinusitis. Catarrhal deafness responds well to Elder Flowers. Elder Berries have similar properties to the Flowers with the addition of their usefulness in rheumatism.

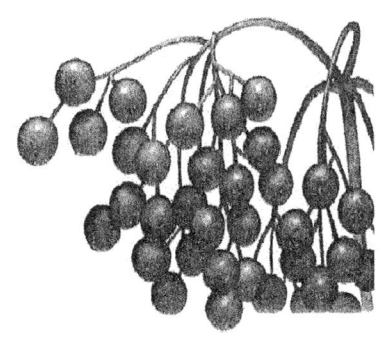

# Ginkgo Biloba

**Botanical Name:** Ginkgo Biloba
**Common Name:** Ginkgo nut, Maidenhair tree
**Parts Used:** Leaves and nut
**System Effected:** Lungs, kidneys; the leaves have been found to be affective for the brain.
**Properties:** Anti-inflammatory, vaso-dilatory, relaxant, digestive bitter, uterine stimulant, improves circulation to the brain.
**Used For:** Traditionally known as an anti-microbial & anti-tubercular agent, new research has shown a profound activity on brain function and cerebral circulation. Clinically it is proving effective in a range of vascular disorders. Improves blood circulation to the brain, improving peripheral blood circulation, coldness, tinnitus, Alzheimer's and senility, to improve one's mood and sociability, Raynaud's disease, arthritic and rheumatic problem, arteriosclerosis, eye weakness caused by poor circulation, vertigo, anxiety and tension, lung and bronchial congestion.

# Ginger

**Botanical Name:** Zingiber Officinale
**Common Name:** Ginger
**Parts Used:** The rootstock
**System Effected:** Stomach, liver, lungs, circulation
**Properties:** Stimulant, carminative, anti-spasmodic, rubefacient, diaphoretic, emmenagogue.
**Used For:** Ginger may be used as a stimulant of the peripheral circulation in cases of bad circulation, chilblains and cramps. In feverish conditions, Ginger acts as a useful diaphoretic, promoting perspiration. As a gargle it may be effective in the relief of sore throats. Externally it is the base of many fibrosis's and muscle sprain treatments. Ginger has been used world-wide as an aromatic carminative and pungent appetite stimulant. In India, and in other countries with hot and humid climates, ginger is eaten daily and is a well-known remedy for digestion problems. Its wide-spread use is not only be due to flavor, but to the anti-oxidant and anti-microbial effects, necessary for preservation of food, essential in such climates.

# Ginseng

**Botanical Name:** Panax Ginseng
**Common Name:** Ginseng
**Parts Used:** Root
**System Effected:** Heart and circulation; general effects on the whole body
**Properties:** Alternative, Cardiac tonic, hepatic tonic, Stimulant.
**Used For:** Ginseng is considered the king of all tonics. It provides a stimulation to the entire body energy to overcome stress and fatigue and to recover from weakness and deficiencies. Ginseng has a very beneficial effect on the heart and circulation and used to normalize blood pressure, reduce blood cholesterol and prevent arteriosclerosis. It nourishes the blood and is thus used to treat anemia. By reducing blood sugar levels, it is useful in managing diabetes.

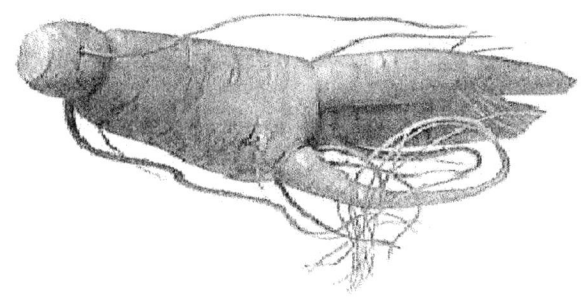

# Green Tea Leaf

**Botanical Name:** Camellia sinensis
**Common Name:** Green tea
**Parts Used:** Young leaves and leaf buds
**System Effected:** Liver, heart, cancer fighting
**Properties:** Stimulant, diuretic, astringent
**Used For:** Green tea contains extremely powerful antioxidants, a range of catechins in particular, which protect against health problems such as cancer and cardiovascular disease. It also contains varying amounts of caffeine bound to tannins; the caffeine content depends on where the tea is grown. For some types of tea, the caffeine content is comparable to that of coffee. However, even the green teas with the highest caffeine content are much gentler on the body and the adrenals than coffee, the reason being that the caffeine is bound to the tannins in the tea, which ensures a somewhat slower rush of caffeine into the blood. The result is a much gentler and more sustained energy boost, compared to coffee and black tea. Also, you won't experience the energy downs you get from coffee, when the rush of caffeine suddenly stops as abruptly as it started. So for those having trouble getting through the day without coffee, which stresses the body's biochemistry, green tea is not merely an alternative, but an improvement. It can do what you want from coffee, but it has none of the negative effects.
Green tea also seems to increase fat oxidation to a level greater than what can be explained by its caffeine

content alone. So green tea might also be good for weight loss when combined with a proper diet. The tannins in green tea have a beneficial effect on the GI flora; they inhibit the growth of pathogenic bacteria in the GI tract. One Japanese study showed antibacterial and even bactericidal effect against some types of pathogenic bacteria, which might attack the GI tract. Green tea might also be a possible agent for maintaining remission in patients with an inflammatory bowel disease, because of its powerful ant microbial and antioxidant properties. Quite a few people have a horrible experience the first time they drink green tea and thus shun it from then on.

# Guarana Berry

**Botanical Name:** Paullinia Cupana
**Common Name:** Brazilian cocoa
**Parts Used:** Crushed seeds
**System Effected:** Kidney and adrenals
**Properties:** Stimulant, nervine, aphrodisiac, febrifuge.
**Used For:** From the tannin it contains it is useful for mild forms of leucorrhoea, diarrhea, etc., but its chief use in Europe and America is for headache, especially if of a rheumatic nature. It is a gentle excitant and serviceable where the brain is irritated or depressed by mental exertion, or where there is fatigue or exhaustion from hot weather. Its benefit is for nervous headache or the distress that accompanies menstruation, or exhaustion following dissipation. It is not recommended for chronic headache or in cases where it is not desirable to increase the temperature, or excite the heart or increase arterial tension. Dysuria often follows its administration. It is used by the Indians for bowel complaints, but is not indicated in cases of constipation or blood pressure.

# Licorice Flower

**Botanical Name:** Glycyrrhiza Glabra
**Common Name:** Licorice
**Parts Used:** Roots
**System Effected:** Endocrine system, liver, lungs
**Properties:** Expectorant, demulcent, anti-inflammatory, anti-hepatotoxic, anti-spasmodic, mild laxative.
**Used For:** Licorice is a traditional herbal remedy with an ancient history and world wide usage. Modern research has shown it to have effects upon, amongst other organs, the endocrine system and liver. This is possibly the basis of the herbs anti-inflammatory action. As an anti-hepatotoxic it can be effective in the treatment of chronic hepatitis and cirrhosis, for which it is been widely used in Japan. Much of the liver orientated research has focused upon the tri terpene glycyrrhizin. Glycyrrhizin inhibits the growth of several DNA and RNA viruses, inactivating Herpes simplex virus particles irreversibly. It has a wide range of uses in bronchial problems such as catarrh, bronchitis and coughs in general. Licorice is used in allopathic medicine as a treatment for peptic ulceration, a similar use to its herbal use in gastritis and ulcers. It can be used in the relief of abdominal colic.

# Pau D'arco

**Botanical Name:** Tabebuia heptaphylla
**Common Name:** Tabebuia, Lapacho, Purple lapacho
**Parts Used:** Inner bark of the tree
**System Effected:** Blood, liver, lungs
**Properties:** Alternative, antifungle, hypotensive, antidiabetic, bitter tonic, digestive, antibacterial, Antitumor.
**Used For:** Slowing and inhibiting the growth of cancer and tumors, for skin diseases. Pau D'arco seems to first eliminate the pain caused by the disease and then multiply the number of red corpuscles. Thus the range of its curative action is phenomenal. It is good for ulcers, diabetes, rheumatism, osteo-myelitis, leukemia, various cancers, ringworm, bronchitis and other respiratory problems.

# Peppermint

**Botanical Name:** Mentha Piperita
**Common Name:** Peppermint
**Parts Used:** Leaf
**System Effected:** Digestive system
**Properties:** Carminative, anti-inflammatory, anti-spasmodic, aromatic, diaphoretic, anti-emetic, nervine, anti-microbial, analgesic.
**Used For:** Peppermint is an excellent carminative, having a relaxing effect on the muscles of the digestive system, combats flatulence and stimulates bile and digestive juice flow. It is used to relieve intestinal colic, flatulent dyspepsia and associated conditions. It helps to relieve the nausea & vomiting of pregnancy and travel sickness. Peppermint can play a role in the treatment of ulcerative conditions of the bowels. It is a traditional treatment of fevers, colds and influenza. As an inhalant it is used as temporary relief for nasal catarrh. Where headaches are associated with digestion, Peppermint may help. As a nervine it eases anxiety and tension. In painful periods, it relieves the pain and eases associated tension. Externally it is used to relieve itching and inflammations.

# Passion Flower

**Botanical Name:** Passiflora Incarnata
**Common Name:** Passion Fruit
**Parts Used:** Leaves and whole plant.
**System Effected:** Heart, Liver
**Properties:** Nervine, hypnotic, anti-spasmodic, anodyne, hypotensive.
**Used For:** Passiflora has a depressant effect on Central Nervous System activity and is hypotensive; they are used for their sedative and soothing properties, to lower blood pressure, prevent tachycardia and for insomnia. The alkaloids and flavonoids have both been reported to have sedative activity in animals. Many of the flavonoids, such as apigenin, are well-known. For pharmacological activity, particularly anti-spasmodic and anti-inflammatory activities. It is the herb of choice for treating insomnia. It aids the transition into a restful sleep without any 'narcotic' hangover. It may be used wherever an anti-spasmodic is required, e.g. in Parkinson's disease, seizures and hysteria. It can be very effective in nerve pain such as neuralgia and the
viral infection such as shingles. It may be used for tension and spasmodic activity in asthma.

# Healing Teas for Common Ailments

**Acne:** Dandelion tea, Chickweed tea, Burdock tea, any of theses teas help to purify and cleanse the blood.

**Allergies:** Parsley tea with a teaspoon of Bee Pollen.

**Anemia:** Dandelion tea, Yellow Dock tea Dandelion contains the nutritive salts necessary to build good blood. Yellow Dock is very high in natural iron.

**Appetite:** Alfalfa tea, Chamomile, and Peppermint tea. Theses teas help to improve the appetite.

**Arteriosclerosis:** Hawthorn tea and Rose Hip tea.

**Arthritis:** Ginger tea, Burdock tea, Yucca Root tea Burdock reduces the swelling in the joints. Ginger tea in nature's viox. Yucca contains steroids and will reduce inflammation in the Joints.

**Asthma:** Lobelia tea with honey. Lobelia is used during an acute attack.

**Bad Breath:** Parsley tea with cloves. Green tea drinks are very helpful add a clove or two to spice it up.

**Blood Purifier:** Red Clover tea, Yarrow, Burdock tea, any of theses teas help to purify and cleanse out the blood.

**Boils:** Dandelion, Burdock and Red Clover tea. Taken as a infusion will help cleanse the body of boils.

**Bronchitis:** Pleurisy Root tea, Ginger tea with Cayenne. Ginger tea with a little Cayenne helps clean out the bronchial tubes.

**Burns:** Aloe Vera tea. Taken internally will help cool down the body.

**Cancer:** Pau D'arco and Red clover tea. Helps to build your immune system up.

**Childbirth:** Blue Cohosh and Red Raspberry tea. Helps to strengthen the uterus and tone the reproductive organs.

**Circulation:** Ginger tea with Gingko Biloba. Helps to improve the circulation.

**Cleansing:** Dandelion tea or Chickweed tea. Theses teas help to cleanse out your stomach.

**Constipation:** Cascara Sagrada, Slippery Elm, Psyllium, Cascara Sagrada will improve bowel tone bring about a beneficial effect.

**Cough:** Licorice tea, Comfrey tea or Lobelia. Licorice is great to calm and sooth your throat.

**Diabetes and Pancreas:** Golden Seal tea with Uva Ursi.

**Diarrhea:** Raspberry, Slippery Elm and Nutmeg.

**Digestive Problems:** Ginger tea with Fennel Seeds and Peppermint Leaves.

**Energy:** Ginseng tea with Bee Pollen & Alfalfa.

**Fever:** Rose Hips with Catnip will help lower fevers.

**Flu:** Golden Seal, Ginger, Peppermint & Echinacea tea.

**Gas:** Ginger tea is wonderful to settle the stomach.

**Headache:** Thyme & Black Cohosh are great for pains.

**Insomnia:** Kava Kava or Valerian Root tea.

**Kidney/Bladder:** Uva Ursi & Parsley tea.

**Liver:** Dandelion tea with some lemon.
**Lungs:** Comfrey or Pleurisy Root with Fenugreek tea.

**Lymph & Swollen Glands:** Echinacea and Golden Seal.

**Menstrual Pain:** Chamomile tea calms stomach cramps.

**Nausea:** Red Raspberry tea.

**Nervous Disorders:** Passion Flower with Chamomile.

**Obesity:** Chickweed tea with a teaspoon of Kelp powder.

**Parasites:** Black Walnut tea with Chamomile & Sage.

**Pituitary Gland:** Gotu Kola with Alfalfa.

**Sexual:** Ginseng tea with Cinnamon, Cloves & Damiana.

**Skin Problems:** Red Clover tea with Chickweed.

**Spleen:** Dandelion tea with Yellow Dock.

**Thyroid & Goiter:** Brew some Kelp Tea.

**Tumors:** Red Clover tea with Pau D'arco.

**Varicose Veins:** White Oak Bark.

**Wounds/Bruises/Sores:** Aloe Vera juice or Slippery Elm.

# Fun Tea Recipes

**Meditation Tea**
4 cups boiling water.
6 herbal tea bags (chamomile& peppermint)
1/4 cup turbinado
2 tbsp. lemon juice
In teapot, pour boiling water over tea bags; cover and steep 5 minutes. Remove tea bags; stir in sugar and lemon juice. Garnish, if desired, with lemon slices.

**Tea Punch**
1/2 pint Golden Green tea
6 oz. turbinado
1/2 pint orange squash
4 tbsps. lemon juice
2 small bottles ginger ale
1 large bottle lemonade
1 orange, sliced
Put the hot tea in a bowl, add the sugar and stir until dissolved. Add the orange squash and lemon juice and strain. Chill. Just before serving mix in the ginger ale, lemonade and orange slices. Serves 12 people.

**Rose Petal Tea**
2 c. firmly packed fragrant rose petals (15 large roses, wash and pat dry)1 c. tea leaves Preheat oven to 200. Place rose petals on an ungreased baking sheet. Leaving oven door slightly open, dry petals in oven for 3 to 4 hours or

until completely dry, stirring occasionally. In a food processor, fitted with steel blade, process rose petals and tea leaves until finely chopped. Store in airtight container. To brew tea: Place 1 teaspoon tea for each 8 ounces of water in a warm teapot. Bring water to a boil and pour over tea. Steep 5 mins., stir & strain. Serve hot or chilled. Serves 3.

**Almond Tea**
4 Tea bags your favorite tea
1/2 tsp Lemon zest, finely grated
4 cups Boiling water
1/2 cup turbinado
2 tbs Lemon juice
1 tsp Almond extract
1/4 tsp Vanilla
Steep tea and lemon rind in boiling water for about 5 minutes. Stir in turbinado, lemon juice, almond and vanilla. Serve hot

**Tea Egg Nog**
6 Tea bags, your favorite tea.
2 Eggs
14 oz Sweetened condensed milk
1 tsp Vanilla
1/4 tsp Salt
1 quart Milk
1/2 pint Whipping cream
Ground nutmeg
Brew all 6 tea bags in 1 cup of water. Steep for 5 minutes and remove bags. Let the tea cool, then add eggs (beaten), both milks, vanilla, salt, and mix well. Serve, with whipped

cream and nutmeg for garnish. Serves 8.

## Russian Tea

2 tablespoons black tea.
4 cups boiling water.
1/2 cup berry jam.
4 thin slices of lemon.
Place the loose tea in a pre-warmed teapot. Pour in the boiling water, and let tea steep for 5 minutes. Meanwhile, place a well-rounded tablespoon of raspberry jam in each clear glass cup or mug. Strain the tea into each glass, and top with a lemon slice.

## Indian Tea Milk

For one quart:
2 cups water 3-4 whole cloves 1 stick cinnamon
3-4 cardamom pods (cracked open)
Bring these to a boil; let stand as long as possible.
Then add to: 1/4 cup loose black tea (or 4 tea bags) and let steep. Then add: 2 cups milk to the tea-spice mixture and heat but do not boil. When hot, strain and add: 4 tablespoons of turbinado.
(or a little less) stir and keep hot.

## Hot Tea Punch

5 bags of your favorite tea
6 cups water
3/4 cup turbinado
2 cinnamon sticks
8 whole cloves
1 1/2 cups orange juice 1/3 cup fresh lemon juice. Bring first 4 ingredients to boil in heavy large saucepan over

high heat, stirring until sugar dissolves. Boil 6 minutes. Remove from heat. Add tea bags. Cover and let steep 10 minutes. Discard tea bags. Add orange and lemon juices to punch. (Can be prepared 1 day ahead. Cover and refrigerate. Re - warm before continuing.) Using slotted spoon, remove whole spices. Serve hot.

**Spearmint tea**
1 - cup turbinado
1 - pint water
1/4 - cup spearmint leaves
3 - teaspoon loose tea
1 - lemon, juice

Stir turbinado and water in a saucepan. Bring water to a boil. In another saucepan, combine spearmint and tea leaves. Steep for 15 minutes. Remove the spearmint and tea leaves and let is cool.

When cool, add the lemon juice and pour in enough water to make 1/2 gallon of tea. You can serve the tea either hot or cold.

**Indian Chai tea**
3 teabags black tea
4 cups water
1 3 inch cinnamon stick
1 inch piece of ginger root cut into 4 slices
1/2 tsp (2 ml) cardamom seeds
1/2 tsp (2 ml) black peppercorns
1/2 tsp (2 ml) whole cloves
1 tsp (5 ml) whole coriander seeds
1 cup (225 ml) milk
honey or other sweetener to taste

Put tea bags, cinnamon sticks, cloves, ginger and turbinado into a large teapot. Pour boiling water over and allow to steep 3 minutes. Remove tea bags and steep for 5 minutes. To serve, pour tea into cups and float a quarter slice of orange in each cup.

## Ginger Spice Tea
1 Ginger Root peeled & grated
2 Pieces (3" ea) cinnamon Sticks
8 Whole cloves
6 cup Boiling water
2 Orange slices
Put grated ginger, cinnamon sticks, cloves, ginger and turbinado into a large pan with water. Let it boil for 30 minutes. To serve, pour tea into cups and float a quarter slice of orange in each cup.

## Lavender Sun Tea
6 - tea bags
1 cup of dried Lavender
1 ½ - quarts cold water
In a 2-quart class contain (best to be clear) add water and tea bags. Cover container and place in sunlight or at room temperature for 2-3 hours or longer. Brewing length depends on the strength you desire. Remove tea bags and store in refrigerator. Serves 8.

# Glossary of Tea Terms

**agony of the leaves:** expression describing the unfurling of rolled or twisted leaves during steeping.

anhui: one of the major black tea producing regions in China.

**aroma:** fragrant flavor of brewed leaf, consisting of the essential oils of tea.

**assam:** Tea grown in the state of Assam, in India. These (generally black) teas are known for their strong, deep red infusions.

**astringency:** the drying sensation in the mouth caused by teas high in unoxidized polyphenols.

**autumnal:** tea produced late in the growing season.

**bakey:** tea taster expression for over fired teas.

**bergamot:** essential oil of the bergamot orange used to flavor a black tea base to make Earl Grey tea.

**billy:** Australian term referring to tin pot with wire handle to suspend over an open fire in which tea is boiled.

**biscuity:** tea taster's expression, often used with Assam teas that have been fired well but not overly so.

**black:** the most common form of tea worldwide. prepared from green tea leaves which have been allowed to oxidize, or ferment, to form a reddish brew.

**blend:** mixture of teas, usually to promote consistency between growing seasons.

**bloom:** tea taster's term to describe sheen or luster present to finished leaf.

**body:** tea taster's term to denote a full strength brew.

**bold:** large leaf cut tea.

**brassy:** unpleasant acidic bite from improperly withered tea.

**break:** auction term referring to a lot for sale, usually 18 chests or more.

**brick tea:** tea leaves that have been steamed and compressed into bricks. Tea is typically shaved and boiled with butter and salt to make a soup.

**bright:** denotes a bright red brew or light leaf, as opposed to a dull brown or black color.

**brisk:** a tea high in astringency. Also a trademarked characteristic of Lipton tea.

**broken:** smaller leaf style usually created during manufacture by passing the leaf through a cutter.

**caffeine:** stimulating compound present in tea.

**cambric tea:** a very weak tea infusion in an excess of milk and sugar.

**catechins:** class of polyphenol present in high concentrations in green tea, but found in varying levels in other teas derived from the tea plant.

**ceylon:** teas made in Sri Lanka.

**cha:** Romanized spelling of Chinese and Japanese character referring to tea.

**chai:** Often refers to masala chai, or spiced tea, a strong black tea infused with milk, sugar, and spices.

**chest:** classical tea package, usually made of wood and aluminum-lines, used to ship tea from plantation.

**chesty:** tea taster's term signifying off odor in tea from the wood in the tea chest.

**chunmee:** a grade of Chinese tea with a curled shape.

**congou:** a general name for Chinese black tea, derived from gongfu.

**coppery:** bright infusion of good quality black tea.

**ctc:** stands for Crush, Tear, and Curl, a machine-based process which macerates the leaves by pressing through counter-rotating rollers to create a stronger, more colorful tea.

**darjeeling:** Tea grown in the Darjeeling region, a mountainous area around the Himalayas, of India. These (generally black) teas are well known for their crisp astringency.

**dhool:** refers to the tea leaf during fermentation, noted for its coppery color.

**dust:** the smallest grade of tea, this is typically associated with lower quality, but is prized for its quick extraction and is commonly used in teabags.

**earl grey:** Black tea that is scented with the essential oil of bergamot, a citrus.

**fanning:** small, grainy particles of leaf sifted out of better grade teas.

**fermentation:** used in the process of preparing black and oolong tea, this step involves allowing the natural browning enzymes present in tea leaf to oxidize fresh green tea leaves and to impart the darker brown-red color and characteristic aroma.

**fibrous:** teas which contain a large percentage of fanning.

**firing:** the process of rapidly heating the leaf, either with hot air or in a wok, to quickly halt fermentation and dry the leaf to its final product.

**flat:** teas lacking astringency or briskness.

**flowery:** used in grading the size of tea, it typically indicates a leaf style with more of the lighter colored tips.

**flush:** the freshly-picked tea leaves, typically comprising the bud and first two leaves of the growing tea shoot.

**formosa:** tea produced in Taiwan, typically oolong teas.

**full:** strong tea without bitterness and possessing good color.

**genmaicha:** green tea with toasted rice.

**golden:** denoting the orange colored tip present in high quality black tea.

**gong fu:** meaning performed with care, this typically refers to a style of brewing with many repeated short infusions.

**gongfu:** meaning performed with care, this typically refers to a style of brewing with many repeated short infusions of leaf in a miniature pot.

**grainy:** term used to describe high quality CTC teas.
green: unfermented, dried tea, more commonly found in China and Japan.

**gunpowder:** a green tea which is rolled into pellets which unfurl in hot water.

**gyokuro:** Japanese green tea produced from shaded plants. "Pearl Dew".

**hard:** pungent tea, desired in some Assam teas.

**harsh:** bitter teas.

**heavy:** a thick, colorful infusion with little briskness or astringency.

**hyson:** Chinese green teas. Brand of tea in common usage during 18th century. "flourishing spring".

**jasmine:** black tea scented with jasmine flowers, typically made with green Pouchong tea as the base.

**keemun:** black tea from central China, typically hand rolled and fired.

**lapsang souchong:** A Chinese black tea which is fired (dried) over a smoky (pine wood) fire to impart its characteristic smoky flavor.

**light:** liquor lacking body or thickness.

**malty:** slightly over-fired tea, sometimes desirable.

**metallic:** tea taster's term to denote coppery taste of some teas.

**muddy:** tea taster's term to denote a dull, blackish color of the infusion.

**nose:** the aroma of the tea.

**oolong:** A form of tea characterized by lighter brews and larger leaf styles. This tea is typically understood as a lightly fermented tea, between green and black tea on a continuum.

**orange pekoe:** Referring to size of leaf, not quality or flavor, this term indicates a larger-size grade of whole leaf teas.

**orthodox:** prepared using a technique which leads to larger leaf styles mirroring hand-produced teas.

**pan fired:** tea that is steamed and then agitated in an iron wok over a fire.

**pekoe:** derived from baihao, the white hairs of the new buds on the tea shrub, this term currently refers to the smaller-size grade of whole leaf teas.

**plain:** tea taster's term to denote dull liquor with sour taste.

**plucking:** the process of harvesting the tea by cutting the flush from the growing tea shrub.

**polyphenols:** astringent compounds present in tea.

**puerh:** a type of tea most notably from the Yunnan province of China. Damp green tea that has been fermented microbiologically to a black leaf.

**pungent:** tea taster's term to denote a very astringent tea.

**rawness:** bitter taste

**rolling:** the process of crushing the leaves to initiate fermentation and impart twist.

**self drinking:** rounded, well bodied tea that can be served unblended.

**smoky:** tea taster's term for teas that have been fired over smoky flames, imparting a smoky flavor.

**soft:** tea taster's term for under fermented teas.

**souchong:** term for large leaf teas derived from the third and fourth leaf of the tea shoot.

**stalk:** describes teas with presence of red stalk pieces from a hard plucking.

**tannin:** erroneous term referring to the astringent polyphenols of tea, unrelated to tannic acid polyphenols of other plants.

**tarry:** tea taster's term for teas that have been fired over smoky flames, imparting a smoky flavor.

**tat:** shelf made of wire mesh or burlap used to spread the leaves out for withering and fermentation

**thea flavins:** orange red polyphenols unique to fermented teas such as black tea, and formed from the condensation of two catechins.

**theanine:** unique amino acid in tea.

**theine:** synonym for caffeine.

**ti kuan yin:** "Iron Goddess of Mercy"- a distinctive type of oolong tea typically longer-fermented and possessing a darker-colored but fragrant brew.

**tippy:** teas with white or golden tips, indicating high quality.

**tisane:** teas produced from the leaves of plants other than the tea plant, herbal tea.

**tuocha:** bowl tea. A form of brick tea comprised of pu-erh tea pressed into a bowl shaped cake.

**twist:** Before fermentation, the leaves need to be crushed to initiate oxidation. This imparts the curled appearance of the finished leaf.

**two and a bud:** the ideal plucked tea for production, consisting of the new tea shoot and the first two leaves.

**white:** a special type of green tea. Distinguished by the presence of the white hairs of the tea flush (baihao) and a lighter green, almost clear, infusion.

**winey:** mellow quality, characteristic of some Keemun teas which have been given time to age.

**withering:** the first step in production of most teas. Involves letting the fresh leaves wither for some period of time after plucking to reduce moisture content.

**woody:** tea taster's term indicating an undesirable grass or hay flavor in black tea.

**yixing:** pronounced ee-hsing, this region in China is noted for its purple clay, used to produce distinctive unglazed teapots.

**yunnan:** Tea grown in the Yunnan province, in the southwest of China. These black teas are known for their spicy character. This region also produces Puerh tea.

*"If a man has no tea in him, he is incapable of understanding truth and beauty"* - Japanese proverb